PIANO PIECES FOR YOUNG CHILDREN

Compiled and edited by Amy Appleby

Order Number AM967472.
Printed in the EU.

ISBN 978-0-8256-1822-2

Visit Hal Leonard Online at
www.halleonard.com

World headquarters, contact:
Hal Leonard
7777 West Bluemound Road
Milwaukee, WI 53213
Email: info@halleonard.com

In Europe, contact:
Hal Leonard Europe Limited
42 Wigmore Street
Marylebone, London, W1U 2RY
Email: info@halleonardeurope.com

In Australia, contact:
Hal Leonard Australia Pty. Ltd.
4 Lentara Court
Cheltenham, Victoria, 3192 Australia
Email: info@halleonard.com.au

PIANO PIECES FOR YOUNG CHILDREN

COMPOSER'S INDEX

FUN SONGS AND FAVORITES

FOLK SONGS

PIANO PIECES FOR YOUNG CHILDREN

CONTENTS

Ode to Joy

Ludwig van Beethoven

Slowly and evenly

Michael, Row the Boat Ashore

American

Moderately

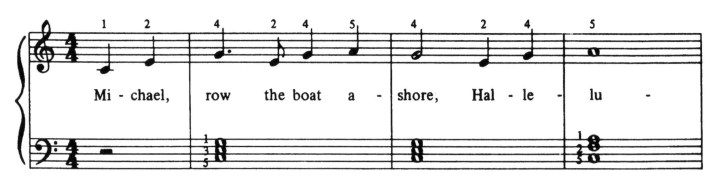

Mi - chael, row the boat a - shore, Hal - le - lu -

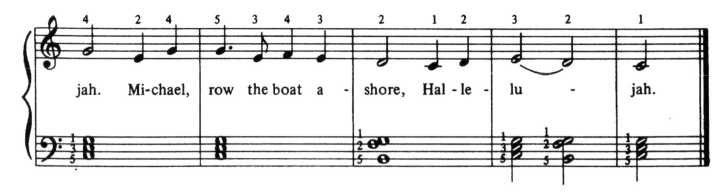

jah. Mi-chael, row the boat a - shore, Hal - le - lu - jah.

Jingle Bells

James Pierpont

Brightly

Jin - gle bells, jin - gle bells, jin - gle all the way.

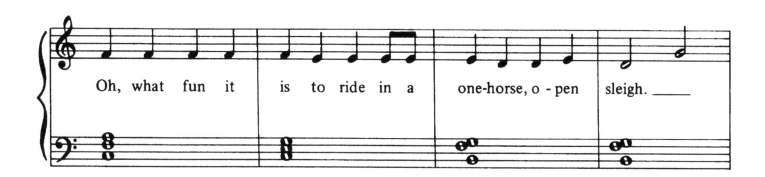

Oh, what fun it is to ride in a one-horse, o - pen sleigh. ____

Jin - gle bells, jin - gle bells, jin - gle all the way.

Oh, what fun it is to ride in a one-horse, o - pen sleigh.

Cowboy Song

Muriel Fouts

Smoothly

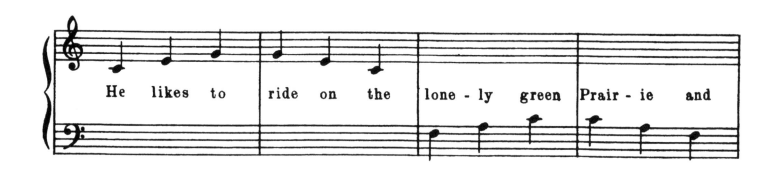

Play with Me

Muriel Fouts

Brightly

Pow Wow

Marie Hill

With a steady beat

For He's a Jolly Good Fellow

English

Lightly

fel - low, For | he's a jol-ly good | fel - low, Which | no-bod-y can de | - ny.

Go Tell Aunt Rhody

American

Slowly and evenly

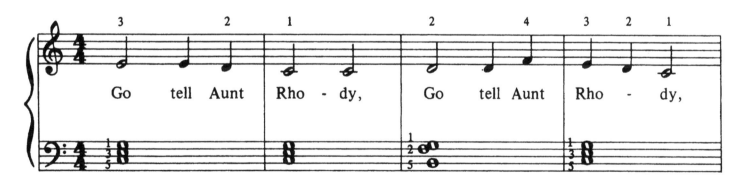

Go tell Aunt Rho - dy, | Go tell Aunt Rho - dy,

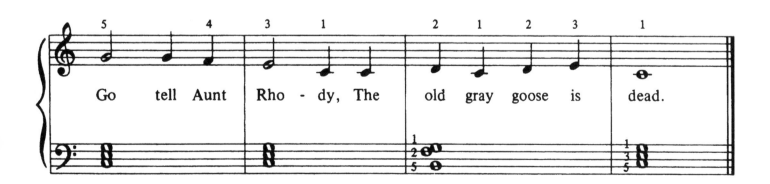

Go tell Aunt | Rho - dy, The | old gray goose is | dead.

Down in the Valley

American

Slowly

Refrain

Little Birdie in a Tree

English

Moderately

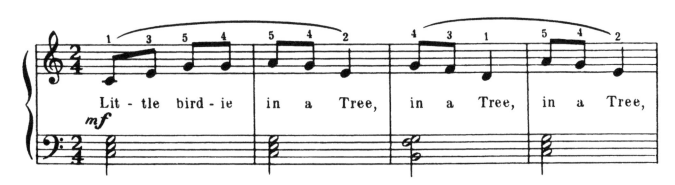

Lit - tle bird - ie in a Tree sing a song for me. *Fine*

D.C.

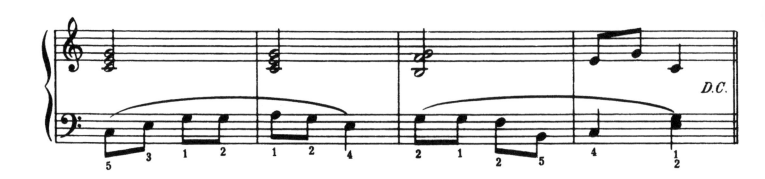

Baa! Baa! Black Sheep

English

Slowly

Baa! Baa! Black sheep have you an-y wool? Yes sir, yes sir, Three bags full, One for my mas-ter And one for my dame, But none for the lit-tle boy that lives in the lane, Baa! Baa! Black sheep have you an-y wool? Yes sir, yes sir, Three bags full.

mf

molto ritard

Bagatelle

Anton Diabelli

Moderately

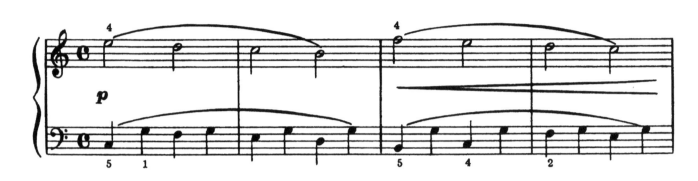

Cradle Song

Carl Heinrich Döring

Moderately

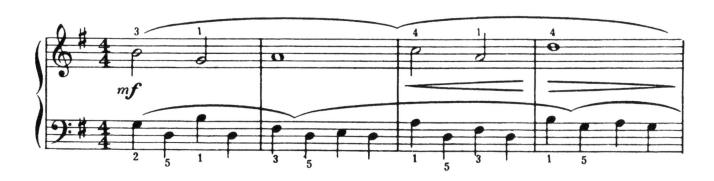

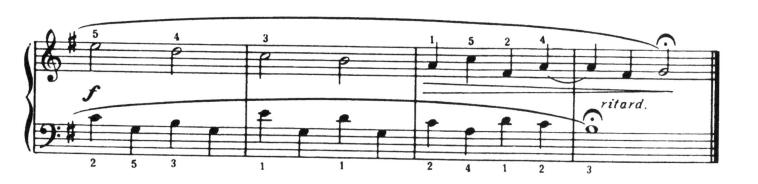

The Mulberry Bush

English

Frère Jacques

French

The Campbells Are Coming

Scottish

Quickly and evenly

Largo
(from *New World Symphony*)

Antonín Dvořák

Slowly and smoothly

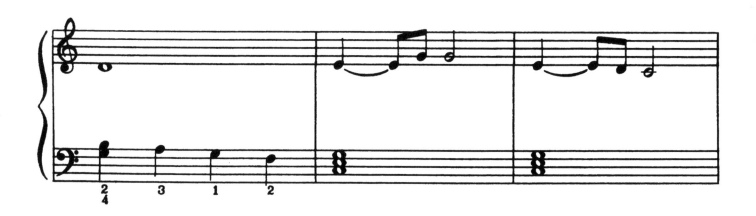

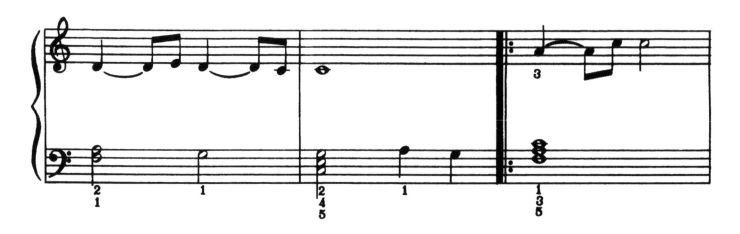

The Thunderer

John Phillip Sousa

Bright march

Caro Nome
(from *Rigoletto*)

Giuseppe Verdi

Moderately

Old Folks at Home

Stephen Foster

Moderately

Good Night Ladies

American

Slowly

Good night la - dies, Good night la - dies,

Good night la - dies, We're goin' to leave you now. *Fine*

Lively

Mer - ri - ly we roll a - long, roll a - long, roll a - long,

Mer - ri - ly we roll a - long o'er the deep blue sea. *D.C.*

Carry Me Back to Old Virginny

James Bland

Moderately

America, the Beautiful

Words by Kathleen L. Bates

Music by Samuel A. Ward

Freely

Oh! Susanna

Stephen Foster

Lively

I__ came to Al - a - ba - ma with my ban - jo on my knee, I'm

g'wan to Lou - si - an - a my__ true love for to see.

f Oh! Su - san - na, oh, don't you cry for me, For I'm

gone to Lou - si - an - a with my ban - jo on my knee.

Oats, Peas, Beans, and Barley Grow

American

Moderately

The Muffin Man

English

Moderately

Polly, Put the Kettle On

English

Quickly

Little Annie Rooney

M. Nolan

Waltz tempo

She'll Be Coming Round the Mountain

American

With a strong and steady beat

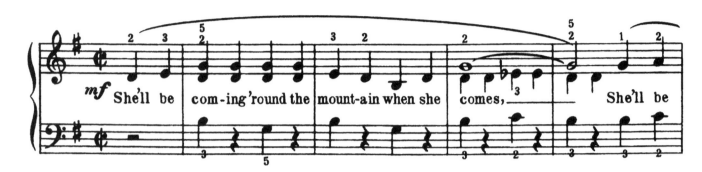

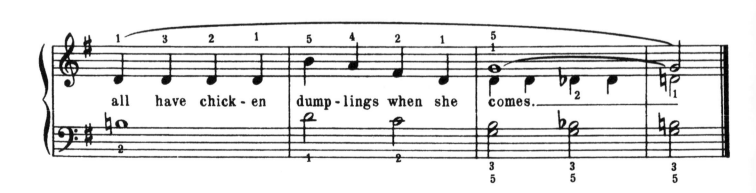

Oh, Dear! What Can the Matter Be?

English

Quickly

In Stilly Night

German

Peacefully

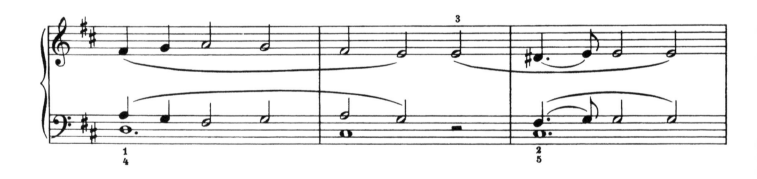

William Tell Overture

Gioacchino Rossini

Brightly

f like a Trumpet call

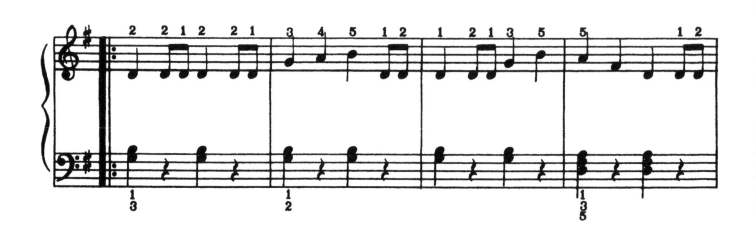

Fine

D. C. al Fine

Greensleeves

English

Moderately slow

Daisy Bell

Harry Dacre

Waltz time

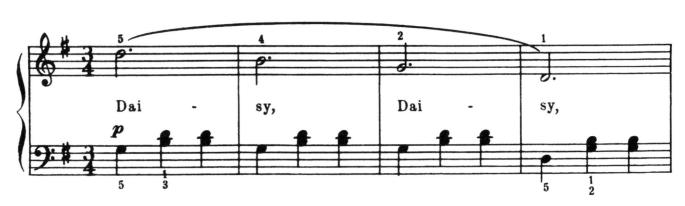

Dai - sy, Dai - sy,

give me your an - swer do

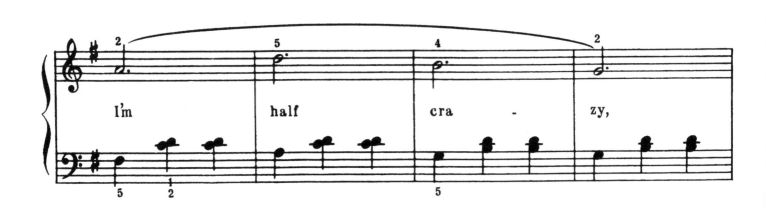

I'm half cra - zy,

Long, Long Ago

Thomas H. Bayley

Moderately

Tell me the Tales that to me were so dear, Long, long a-

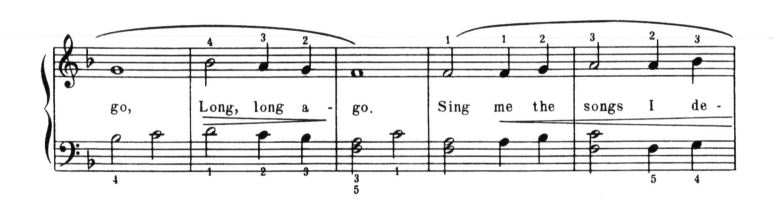

go, Long, long a - go. Sing me the songs I de -

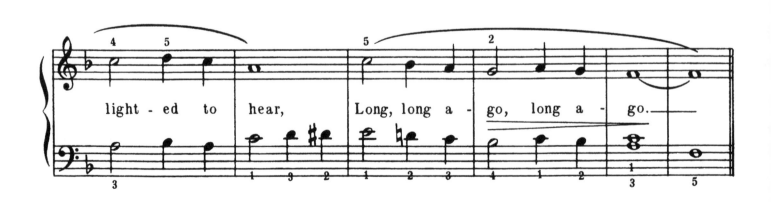

light - ed to hear, Long, long a - go, long a - go.

My Bonnie

Scottish

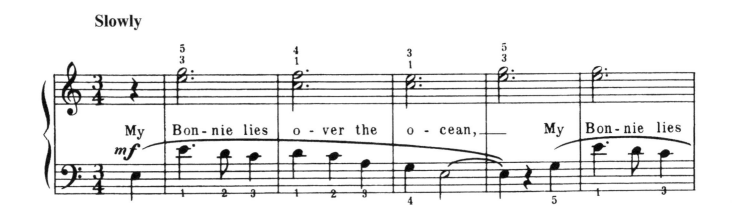

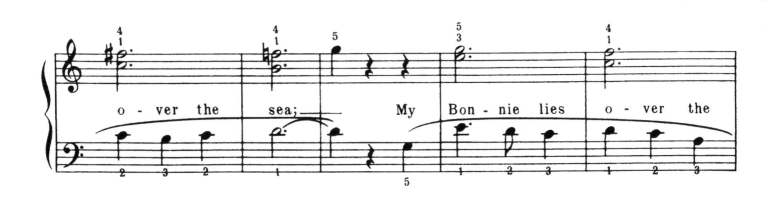

My Old Kentucky Home

Stephen Foster

Moderately

The sun shines bright in the old Ken - tuck - y home, 'Tis

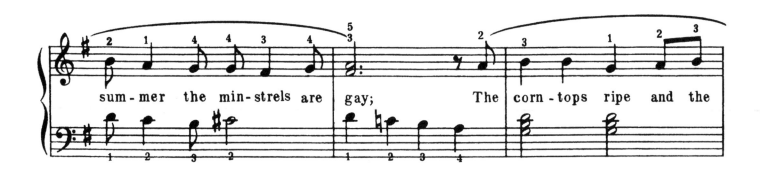

sum - mer the min - strels are gay; The corn - tops ripe and the

mead - ows in bloom, While the birds make mu - sic all the

day. The young folks roll on the lit - tle cab - in floor, All

Blow the Man Down

American

Moderately

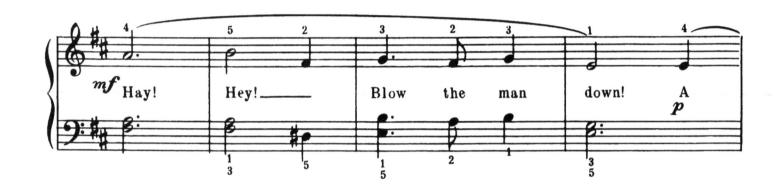

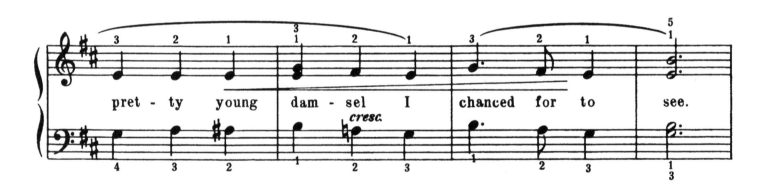

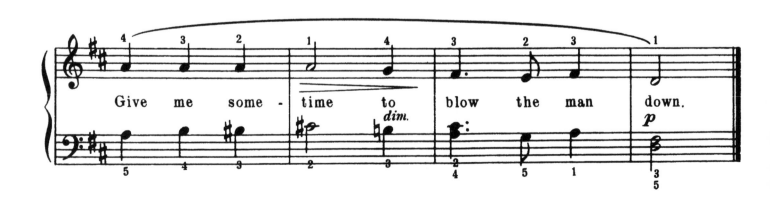

Clementine

American

Moderately

When Johnny Comes Marching Home

American

March tempo

When John-ny comes march-ing home a-gain, Hur - rah!__ hur - rah!__ We'll

give him a heart - y wel - come then Hur - rah,__ hur - rah!__ The

men will cheer, The boys will shout, The la - dies they'll all turn out and we'll

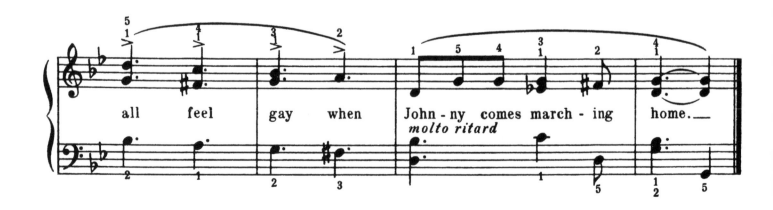

all feel gay when John - ny comes march - ing home.__

molto ritard

Did You Ever See a Lassie?

Scottish

Polly Wolly Doodle

American

March tempo

Turkey in the Straw

American

Moderately fast

Sweet and Low

Joseph Barnby

Over the River and Through the Woods

American

Moderately

Minuet in F

Wolfgang Amadeus Mozart

Lightly

The Stars and Stripes Forever

John Philip Sousa

March tempo

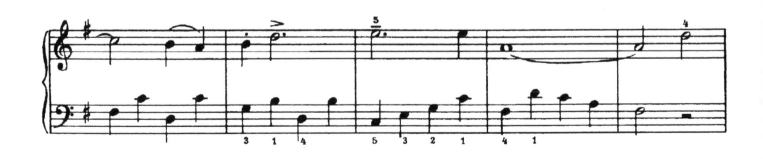

Minnie Waltz

Louis Streabbog

Moderately

Melody

Daniel Gottlob Turk

At a walking pace

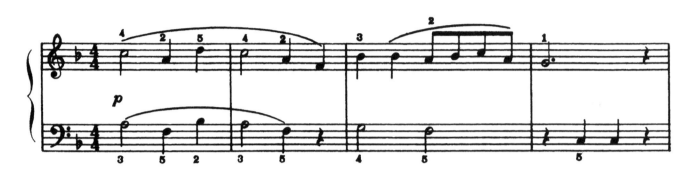

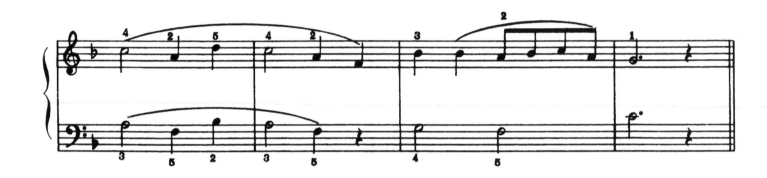

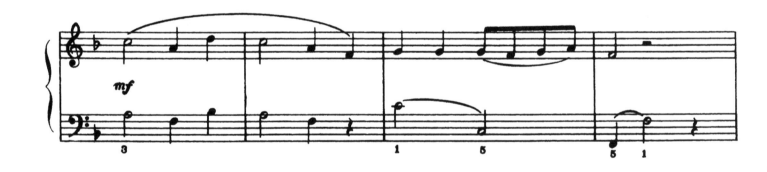

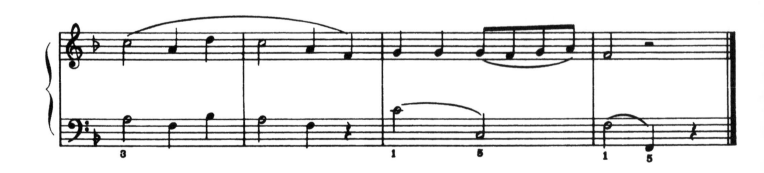

Little German Dance

Ludwig van Beethoven

Moderately

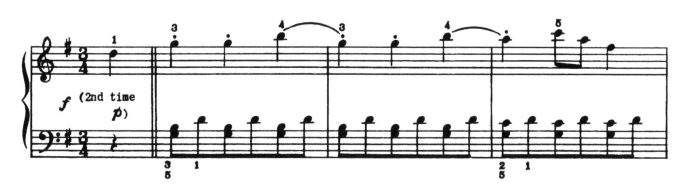

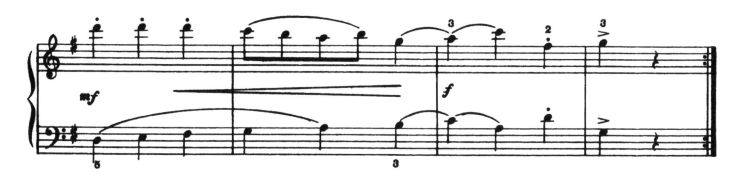

Longing for Spring

Wolfgang Amadeus Mozart

Lullaby

Wolfgang Amadeus Mozart

Moderately

The Caissons Go Rolling Along

E.L. Gruber

March tempo

CHORUS

Arietta

Wolfgang Amadeus Mozart

Slowly

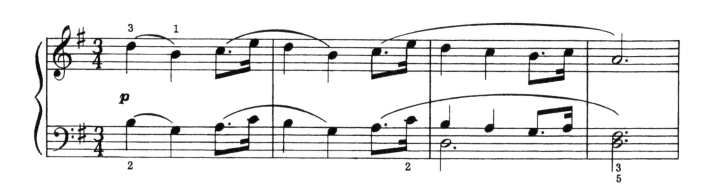

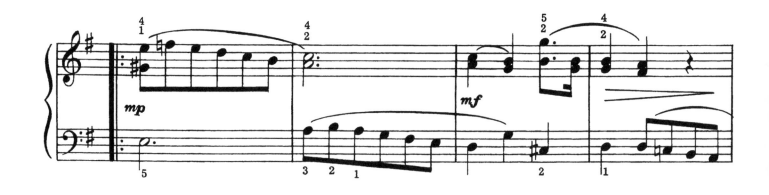

Country Dance

Ludwig van Beethoven

Moderately fast

Juanita

Spanish

Moderately slow

rit. e dim.

Home on the Range

American

At a walking pace

Sonata in A

Wolfgang Amadeus Mozart

Moderately

Rosamunde

Franz Schubert

At a walking pace

Hungarian Dance No. 6

Johannes Brahms

Moderately fast

Evening Star
(from *Tannhäuser*)

Richard Wagner

Moderately slow

Air in B-Flat

Wolfgang Amadeus Mozart

Moderately

In a Little French Village

Peter Ilyich Tchaikovsky

With feeling

The New Doll

Peter Ilyich Tchaikovsky

Moderately slow

Distant Bells

Louis Streabbog

Moderately slow

Dance in G

Franz Joseph Haydn

Medium fast

Air in D Minor

Henry Purcell

Gracefully

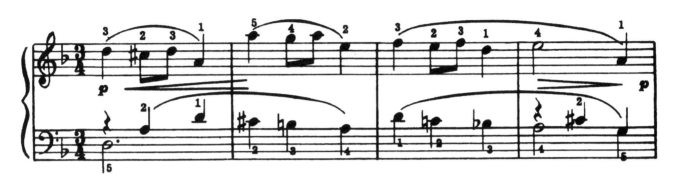

Little Minuet

Jean Philippe Rameau

Medium fast

Allegro in B-Flat

Wolfgang Amadeus Mozart

Medium fast

German Dance

Ludwig van Beethoven

Medium fast

91

Minuet in G Minor

Johann Sebastian Bach

Medium fast

Ecossaise in E-Flat

Ludwig van Beethoven

With spirit

Ecossaise in G

Ludwig van Beethoven

Medium fast

Allegro in F

Franz Joseph Haydn

Dance in F

Franz Joseph Haydn

Medium fast

Minuet in C

Wolfgang Amadeus Mozart

Moderately

Nocturne

Frédéric Chopin

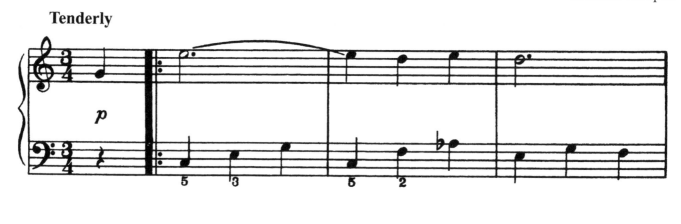

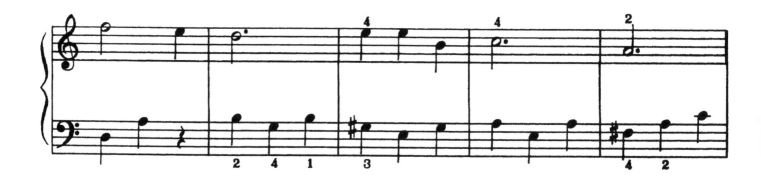

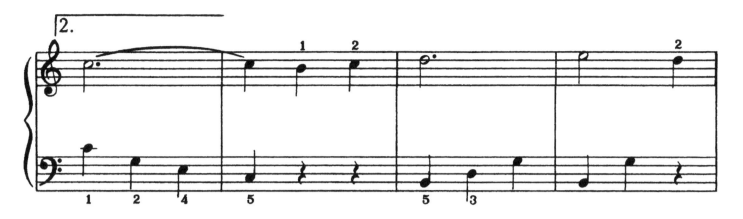

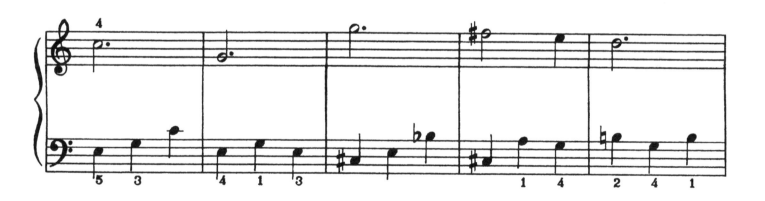

English Jig

Georg Philipp Telemann

Quickly

Sentimental Waltz

Franz Schubert

Italian Song

Peter Ilyich Tchaikovsky

Moderately

il basso sempre staccato

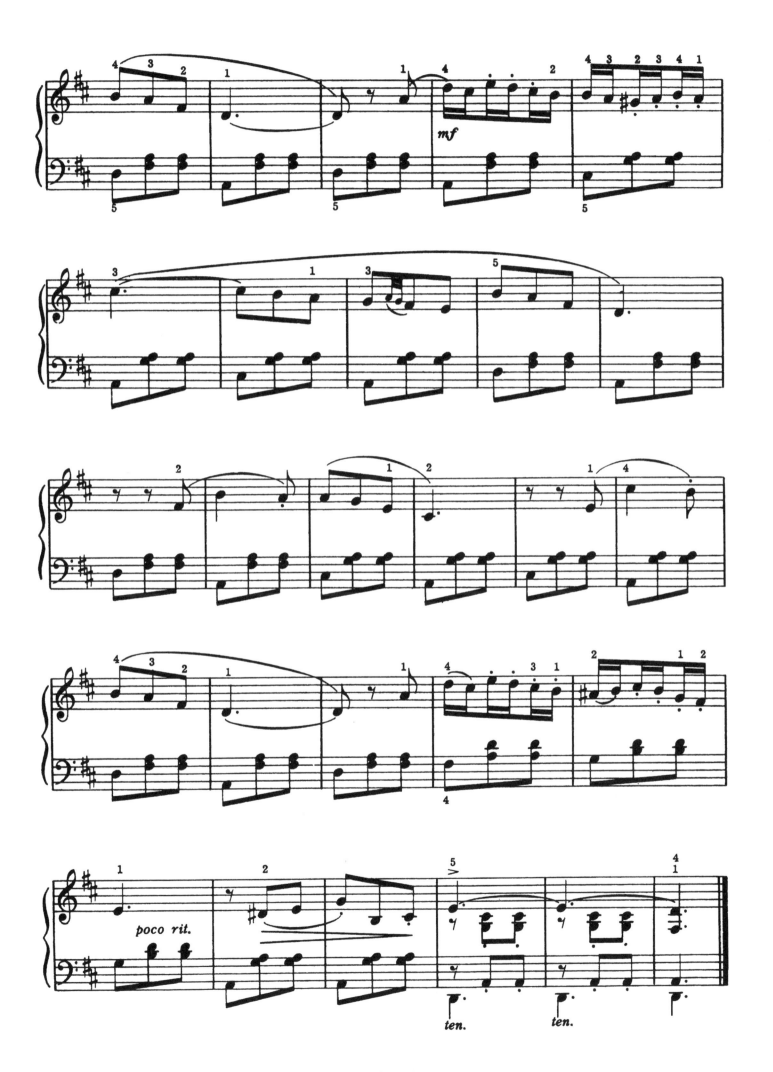

Fantasie Impromptu

Frédéric Chopin

Moderately

Amaryllis

Henri Ghys

Gracefully

D. C. al Fine

Clair de Lune

Claude Debussy

Slowly, with feeling

To a Wild Rose

Edward MacDowell

Tenderly

114

Polovetzian Dance

Alexander Borodin

Moderately

Rêverie

Claude Debussy

Moderately slow

Military Polonaise

Frédéric Chopin

D. C. al Fine

Melody of Love

H. Engelmann

Glow Worm

Paul Lincke

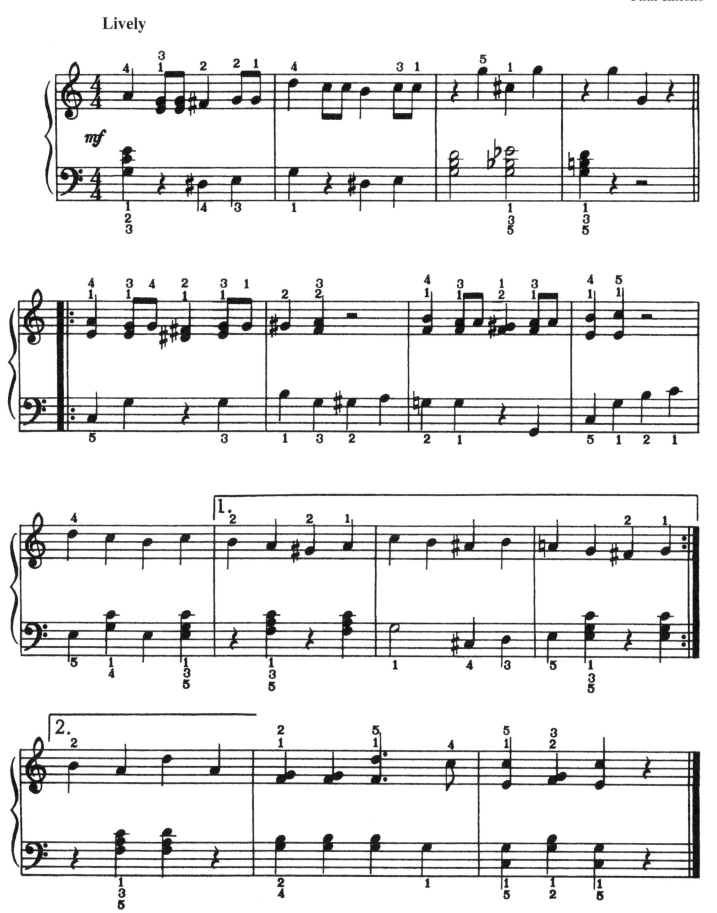

Minuet in D Minor

Johann Sebastian Bach

Slowly and calmly

Musette

Johann Sebastian Bach

Slowly and simply

March Slav

Peter Ilyich Tchaikovsky

Moderately

Santa Lucia

Italian

Slowly

Sonatina

Jean Antoine Andre

Moderately, with movement

Old French Air

French

Moderately

Piano Concerto No. 1

Peter Ilyich Tchaikovsky

Majestically

Symphony Pathétique

Peter Ilyich Tchaikovsky

Slowly, with expression

Liebestraum

Franz Liszt

Majestically

Minute Waltz

Frédéric Chopin

Very fast

Slower

Fine

D. C. al Fine

Hungarian Rhapsody No. 2

Franz Liszt

Slowly

Romeo and Juliet

Peter Ilyich Tchaikovsky

Medium slow

The Irish Washerwoman

Irish

The Sailor's Hornpipe

English

With spirit

Moonlight Sonata

Ludwig van Beethoven

Slowly

Sonata in C

Wolfgang Amadeus Mozart

Piano Pieces for Young Children

NOTES ON THE KEYBOARD

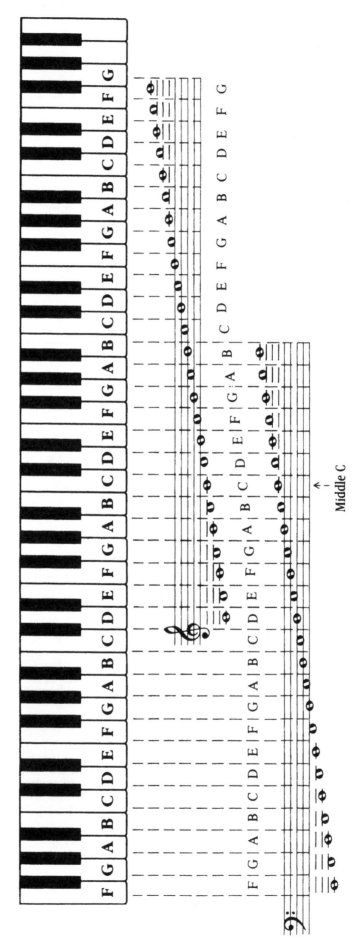

Middle C